AF479834

BLEAK & BLUE

Rendering the Inexpressible Desolation of Depression with a Paintbrush

Written & Illustrated by Kate Ramirez

1 : an act of depressing or a state of being depressed: such as

  a : a state of feeling sad : low spirits : MELANCHOLY

    specifically : a mood disorder that is marked by varying degrees of sadness, despair, and loneliness and that is typically accompanied by inactivity, guilt, loss of concentration, social withdrawal, sleep disturbances, and sometimes suicidal tendencies

But also this:

  b (1) : a reduction in activity, amount, quality, or force

    a *depression* in trade

    (2) biology : a lowering of physical or mental vitality or of functional activity

  c : a pressing down : LOWERING

    a *depression* of the tab key

2   **economics** : a period of low general economic activity marked especially by rising levels of unemployment

    heading towards a *depression*

    periods of economic *depression*

3 : a place or part that is lower than the surrounding area : a depressed place or part : HOLLOW

    The chicken pox left several *depressions* in her skin.

4   **meteorology** : LOW entry 2 sense 1b

    a tropical *depression*

5 a astronomy : the angular distance of a celestial object below the horizon

  b mathematics : the size of an angle of depression

I think it might be time to give the illness a new name.

Things were a mess before they became...less messy.

I can explain...

About 25 years ago, a trip to my doctor's office ended with the unhappy revelation that the chaos in my head was being caused by an illness (absurdly) called depression. The diagnosis didn't evoke much of a reaction from me, I remained as mute, impassive and void of expression as I had when I entered the office. But as the doctor tried to fill the silence with long lists of symptoms and statistics, I quietly wondered how the disease had come to be there (it seems a trivial question but my mind has a talent for distracting itself with the least upsetting aspect of any daunting subject). With apparent relief to have a question to address, the doctor spoke at length of the roles genetics and circumstance play in determining who may end up with the illness. His capacity to provide information far surpassed my rattled mind's ability to absorb it, so when he offered the undemanding task of providing any known family history with depression, I was relieved to take it. I could point to a possible genetic link to the illness rather easily, as even a passing glance at my parents' lives showed that, to a lesser degree, it had affected them both at one point or another. Pinning down circumstance was somewhat trickier. My initial thought was that it likely grew from the fact that, as a couple, my parents were tragically ill-suited.

Individually, my mother and father had enough unresolved psychological mischief floating around to make them immensely creative, interesting and charismatic people. Their start as a couple was infused with far more love than sense, but also with a defiant unwillingness to acknowledge the growth of a slow leak on the love end of things. When my siblings and I were very young, before they decided they sincerely disliked each other, my parents were whimsical and funny, slightly offbeat, very engaging, and very much products of the 1960's. My mother loved Bob Dylan, Pete Seeger, Joan Baez, and everything Marimekko. She sewed her own clothes, she baked leaden bricks of terrifically healthy (and sadly) often inedible bread, she wrote beautifully, she sang beautifully, she played the ukulele, she had a stunningly quick, satirical sense of humor, and a curious obsession with the proper use of grammar. My father was a talented artist, designer and photographer, admired and respected by those he worked with. He was a great teacher, he was an avid gardener, he was humble, he was moody, he was inventive, he had anger management issues. Our family car was a vintage Cadillac hearse that my father had taken a liking to (no joke), and we lived in a house that he converted from a barn, long before that was a thing.

My siblings and I could often be found barefoot and bounding around the tall-grass fields across from our house (sometimes inexplicably in our pajamas). Most of what we did tended towards the creative; we painted pictures with water on the flagstone patio and watched as the sun made them disappear; we built intricate miniature towns out of sticks and leaves and mud and flowers; we found hours of entertainment in a seemingly bottomless trunk of dress-up clothes; we made up games; we performed skits; we built forts.

It was quite a promising beginning. If I could remove all traces of the mental agitation that living through the ugly demise of my parents' relationship had spawned, I would have to describe my early childhood as pretty great. And, if it was possible to cancel out the bad stuff with lots and lots of good stuff, I'd be all set; I would simply be a person with a possible genetic predisposition for depression, but happily lacking the catalyst of circumstance that encourages it to bloom and thrive.

Sadly, all of the lovely quirks that amplified my parents' charms as individuals also served to amplify their ills when they were together, and as a couple they grew to become volatile, combative creatures who loudly and regularly fought with unsettling ferocity. What in the beginning was warm, lighthearted teasing gradually shed its playful quality and morphed into blatant hostility, which by the time I was ten or eleven was on full and regular display. Out of necessity, typical childhood pursuits were shoved aside by the more urgent task of learning to navigate an increasingly nasty emotional battlefield, one that even years of careful observation didn't enable me to completely master. More often than not, my rising belief that no one should be counted on for much of anything – and a sense of self-preservation – drove me to seek solace within the seemingly safer confines of my own head. Without the ability to recognize that there was an alarming amount of unrest brewing in my mind already, and confusing isolation with security, I burrowed deep inside, sprinkled broken glass and thumbtacks across the entrance, and nailed the door shut.

Our family continued scrambling for ways to cope with its spiraling dysfunction until I was about 13 when my mother, having finally had enough, packed up and moved out. As she left, along with half the furniture, she also removed the worn-out illusion that there was someone steering our familial ship. There was no more ship. It was gone, dashed to pieces. We were each of us left drifting around in our own little rudderless dinghy. If I were to guess, I'd have to say that was the point where my emotional development pretty much stalled out, and where it stayed for many decades to follow. Introverted, fearful, often gloomy, kind of prickly, I remained isolated within the confines of my own mind, even as the thoughts it generated became increasingly dire, and my sense of loneliness more profound. If signs of my creeping mental distress were noticed by either of my parents, they were quick to explain them away: I was a hormonal teen, or I was moody like my father, or I was shy, or tired, or hungry, or lacking some other common ingredient needed to sustain normal behavior. (Nothing to see here, move along please).

My growing mental imbalance never incapacitated me. I did all the normal stuff: I finished school, I went to college, I got married, I had kids, I got divorced. I had lots of bad days, sometimes many in a row, but I always managed to keep everything ticking along. It wasn't until I was in my thirties, and the bad days started drastically outnumbering the good days, that I became concerned. When the anxiety, self-doubt, anger and sadness that I was adept at juggling had all seeped together and formed a vast, deep pool that I was increasingly convinced I would drown in, and I started sincerely wishing that I could cease to exist, or at least vanish without leaving behind the grim burden of a suddenly lifeless body, I thought maybe I should find some sort of help.

I went to my GP. He diagnosed me with clinical depression, and advised me to find a good therapist.

I admit that it was mildly heartening to hear there was an illness to blame for my shift from adequately to barely functioning, but I wasn't thrilled to learn that part of its treatment involved examining and discussing the angst that had helped to foster it. Discussing emotions wasn't something we did when I was young. As a child my emotional vocabulary had lodged firmly at the very basic level of happy, sad and angry, and as an adult I had done very little to improve it. The idea that I would be asked to put words to emotions that were so wildly distorted they were no longer recognizable to me was ridiculous. How could I possibly be expected to provide any kind of narrative of the illness when "bad" was the most descriptive word I could produce when asked how I was feeling? It was impossible and I wanted no part of it. The mild relief I experienced on receiving a diagnosis vanished. I drifted back into my increasingly familiar dysfunction and it took an unrelenting effort on the part of my mother and assorted friends to get me to start looking for a therapist.

My mother created a list. By that point my mother had become a therapist, and she had researched and compiled a list of psychiatrists for me to contact in the hopes that I might find one that I liked, or at the very least didn't instantly dislike. I reluctantly made appointments with several of the doctors, but my vague, haltingly mumbled replies to the questions they asked turned every consultation into a humiliating exercise. I began to think that the person I would feel comfortable with, and would somehow be able to explain myself to, simply did not exist. Not wanting to waste any more time trying to achieve the unachievable, I abandoned the list...and its goal. I believed I would never feel at ease in the presence of a therapist, so I simply looked for one whose office was an easy distance from my house, and made an appointment with her via voice mail.

For decades, anger had done the job of keeping me safely distant from a world I had deemed to be teeming with untrustworthy people, and upon meeting the doctor, I quickly tossed her into that same category. I spent each visit to her office pressed into the corner of her sofa with arms crossed like a peevish child enduring a well earned time-out. My trips to her office were making me feel worse than I had been before, and I blamed her for it. She asked questions that made me feel inept and uncomfortable, and the act of trying and repeatedly failing to articulate the magnitude of my emotional distress had only compounded it. She was pushing me to do something that I was unable to do, and I started treating her as if she were my adversary. Each week while the doctor sat across from me in an attitude of calm expectation, I remained fixed behind a meticulously maintained wall of simmering anger. When I dismissed her questions with obvious contempt, she responded with perfectly composed silence. When I spent the good part of an hour staring at the floor, she waited patiently for me to...look elsewhere? Say something? Leave? I didn't know. I stopped caring. I didn't care that I was being impossible. I didn't care that I was showing up at her office once a week for therapy, and at the same time sabotaging every effort she made to help me. I didn't care that we both sat and watched as my hijacked mind skipped further away. But to the doctor's credit she was not easily put off. After many weeks of trying to break through my mute obstinance, she suggested that perhaps I might have more luck translating my thoughts into drawings than I was having with words.

That was a surprise.

I have no idea why, but until that moment I had believed I was enduring the supreme torture of trying to turn chaos into words because somehow *verbal* expression was the only means to any kind of real, medically-sanctioned recovery. In offering me the option of drawing, the doctor graciously handed me a tool I was comfortable using. My struggle had never been with the concept of expression, it had been with the method of expression I was being required to use. Drawing wouldn't exempt me from the task, it would simply provide a less exasperating way of doing it. With an inclination at the time to hate everything, I was mildly puzzled to find that I didn't hate her idea. As unraveled as I was, I reacted with a shrug and a barely audible "maybe"and continued to stare at the floor, but deep within my head I noticed my fading psyche crack a faint, somewhat sardonic smile.

My trips to the therapist always made me want to go to bed. I am a vivid dreamer and depression often made me wish I could finish out what was left of my life drifting through the shifting realms my mind created while I was sleeping. I was rarely depressed in my dreams so sleep was a pretty reliable refuge from the illness, and by association my bed was the place I felt most comfortable. When I returned home from the doctors office, I wandered upstairs, gathered up my drawing supplies, piled them onto my bed and settled myself next to them, perched on a pillow and wrapped in a blanket. I tried to picture the long, silent scream that had been building in my mind since childhood, and briefly wandered through dozens of equally weird and wonderful mental images before a random flash of anger surfaced, wadded them all up and threw them aside. I didn't want weird and wonderful. I wanted stark and brutal. I wanted dark, searing and bleak...I wanted vengeance. I wanted to pin depression to a board like a formaldehyde-soaked frog and dissect it. I wanted to cut it open, unravel its guts and display them with the rest of its grotesque self in a way that left no room for misinterpretation. I wanted to remove the ineffectual verbal descriptions I had so feebly tried to attach to it and create a loud, visual list of all the ways depression screws with your mind. But honestly, I just really, *really* wanted it out of my head. If I could purge it from my person in a form that I could examine from a safe distance, I would call the exercise a success. With a seed of an idea, I reached underneath my bed and blindly groped around for a basket of pamphlets I had been storing there.

My doctor had given me a lot of literature about depression. I didn't read much of it, but I didn't throw it away either. I think I held onto some of the pamphlets in case I needed reminding that I had an illness and not some tragic character flaw. The organizations that had produced the pamphlets ranged from drug companies to non-profit groups, but all of them were written in the same measured, calm, don't-upset-the-crazy-people language that, considering the illness they were warning of, I found more ironic than helpful. The symptoms listed: "Difficulty Concentrating; Persistent Sad or Empty Mood; Excessive Crying" didn't come *even remotely* close to describing what I had been feeling. What did "Excessive Crying"even mean? Who decided what qualified as excessive? Was crying over a happy situation as easily as a tragic one excessive? Was it excessive to tear up for little to no reason at all? Was sobbing uncontrollably over something as mundane as a spilled cup of coffee closer to what was meant? I didn't know, and not knowing really annoyed me. Imagining that a thick slathering of technicolor reality might help to clarify things, I decided my response to the doctor would be to illustrate the pamphlets. And if it accomplished nothing else, at least I would finally have an accurate description of what it looked like inside my head.

I started with Excessive Crying, and with the first successful transfer of mental mayhem to paper I detected the faintest hint of peace.

Progress.

Unfortunately, creating a pile of drawings does not magically cure depression. The illness hung on long after my drawings were finished, but the feel of it had become slightly less… dire. The act of translating depression into pictures had softened some of its more sinister plots, and I no longer felt like it was steering me towards an inescapable, certain end. Tiny wisps of optimism had begun making their way into my head, and, a bit like drinking alcohol after a long, dry period, even a small taste of optimism after so long without it can make you feel somewhat giddy. It can lead you to behave in ways you normally wouldn't. I blame a rogue bit of optimism for all that I did after my drawings were completed. Some time after finishing my drawing project, and with very little forethought, I wrote a letter to William Styron asking if he would consider writing a short piece about depression that I might combine with my drawings to create a book. Quite a surprising move on my part. I usually like to mull an idea over for several years before acting on it. But instead I just went right ahead and did it. And, after the letter was written, I would have found multiple excuses had I simply added it to one of my to-do piles and put off any further steps for another time. But I didn't. I kept right on going. I made copies of my drawings, and I packed them up with the letter and I mailed them to Mr. Styron.

Astonishing.

Not terribly long afterwards, as if to add to my sense of wonder about what I had done, he replied, with a card.

He declined. A firm and decisive no.

I read his note several times. I looked through my drawings, and had to conclude that he had been right to turn me down. Mr. Styron was a celebrated, prize-winning novelist, and I was...me, an unknown person with no accomplishments to speak of, no tangible successes. And I had sent him an unsolicited pile of bizarre drawings. Drawings that most likely made sense only to me. I was mortified. I didn't know what I had been thinking. I started to feel the familiar sensation of a downward spiral tugging at me, and after a seconds-long protest my mind surrendered to it: Mr. Styron was surely out there somewhere laughing at my presumption; a picture book about depression was an asinine idea; I was a pathetic joke, an idiot, a laughably talentless failure, and on and on and on and on...When I had finally blown through my ample stock of self-derision, I gathered up my drawings, arranged them in a neat, orderly stack, placed them in a box, sealed it up and put it in the back of my closet.

Not long after I banished the depression drawings, I started a second project about emotions. It was to be a children's A-Z book, with an emotion for each letter of the alphabet. I made it to the letter U before tarring it with the same self-critical crap, leaving it unfinished and tossing it into the box alongside the first. Out of sight, out of mind. All good. Carry on.

....

As I began feeling better, my focus returned more consistently to the normal stuff that makes up a life. Depression was still lurking around, and it surfaced occasionally to remind me that it had never formally relinquished control, but the days that were lost to it became steadily fewer and less severe. If it wasn't knocking me sideways, I wasn't thinking about it.

I continued to not think about it through many of the years that followed, and only took it up again relatively recently when I moved back to the east coast. As I was unpacking and rifling through stacks of boxes in search of the well-loved objects I needed to make my new surroundings feel less strange, I came upon my box of drawings. Time had not cured me of the habit of quitting mid-way through a project (a fear of failure thing). I was still what my father would have called a half-job; even projects dear to me were abandoned and left as dangling, unfinished thoughts, and there before me were the two that had remained that way the longest. I hadn't seen them, or even thought about them for many years and although genuinely curious to see the children's book illustrations again, I really didn't feel like tackling the depression drawings that were in the box with them. Those needed to wait for another time. I had just moved. I was unpacking. It wasn't the time to go down that particular rabbit hole. They definitely needed to be avoided. So exercising the same level of caution one would use in handling a box of snakes, I cracked the lid just enough to peek inside and grab the kid's book drawings and then snapped it shut again.

Looking through the drawings made two things very clear: I still liked the idea for the book, and there was *absolutely* no question, they were, as my dear mother would have said, awful. They were hastily rendered (not in a good way), unevenly colored and contained several poorly disguised corrections.

They had to be redrawn.

I did redraw them, and it took close to a year. And then I wrote the text. Cue the fireworks, I actually finished the book! I will admit, completing a project was a pretty great feeling.

A few weeks later, with music playing loudly throughout the house, I was happily scrolling through the file of my children's book with a glass of wine, feeling warm and hazy and rather pleased with myself, when it occurred to me; I was in the perfect condition to look at my long-sequestered depression drawings. Cheerful, optimistic and slightly buzzed was surely the perfect emotional cocktail to fend off whatever dregs of misery my stack of drawings might stir up...and, on the off-chance it wasn't, I could always lock them back up again. It was a good plan. And before I could change my mind I ran upstairs and grabbed the box. When I lifted open the lid what greeted me was not the pile of drawings I was expecting, but what looked very much like the contents of a paper recycling bin. Blanketing everything in the box was an odd assortment of small yellow legal sheets, old receipts, used envelopes, and carelessly torn strips of paper. All of which were scribbled over in an agitated, wandering hand that took me a minute to recognize as my own. It was only after I had read through several of the scraps that I remembered what I was looking at: while I was working on the drawings, and during the years my mind was recovering itself, I had written down what I had imagined to be deeply insightful revelations about depression that one day I could pair with my drawings to create some sort of book. The mess of paper I was sorting through was a collection of those notes.

The notes were insightful but not in the way I had thought they would be. Reading them had the same disconcerting effect as very quickly spinning the dial of an old radio, and hearing unintelligible snippets of dozens of voices as it sails through all the stations. The notes were hastily written, unintelligible ramblings that conveyed a state of confused desperation and anger, but little else. Most were incoherent, and many were illegible. The urgency I had felt when I wrote them started coming back, and I remembered lying awake and scribbling them in the dark, and scrambling to find something to write on while sitting in the car, or waiting in a line, or even while brushing my teeth. I remembered thinking how important it was for me to capture it all. And I had.

And it was all nonsense.

The only insight the notes could possibly provide was that depression had made a complete mockery of my mind, but I already knew that. No amount of cheerful wine-infused optimism was sufficient to counter the anxiety that had started to form in my gut, I wasn't ready to jump back into all of that shit. I wasn't prepared. I still had lighthearted children's rhymes skipping around my head. I had simply wanted to flip through my drawings to see if they were the strong, declarative, raised-middle-fingered response to depression that I remembered them to be. Those notes were nothing more than a catalogue of the toxic waste depression had produced while it was occupying my head.

I needed them to go away, and as often happens when my emotional balance is teetering, my first reaction was not my most carefully thought out or mature. I grabbed the hem of my shirt, stretched it out in front of me to form a pouch and began stuffing the notes in by the handful. When the transfer was complete, I clutched the whole mess to my gut with both arms, and awkwardly hurried from room to room looking for some place to hide it all away. It took more than a few minutes and a chance glimpse of myself as I rushed past a mirror to stop the frenzy I was caught in. The sight of myself clutching my overstuffed shirt, while cartoonishly racing about trailing bits of paper in my wake caused me to lose my footing on the wood floor. As my legs flailed around to keep me from falling, the wine and the absurdity of what I was doing hit me simultaneously and produced a burst of laughter that sent the contents of my shirt flying into the air. The notes scattered in all directions. And then paused. Seemingly buoyed by the sudden lightness in the room, they appeared to float in place for half a second before slowly drifting and swirling around each other on their way to the floor.

Still laughing I collapsed in the middle of the scattered mess, and after successfully driving away the panic my laughter slowly trailed off. When it had gone, I gathered the notes into a loose pile, and started reading. I read each one. I put aside the very few that were intelligible, thanked the rest for their efforts and tossed them in the trash.

Returning to close up the box, I found what I thought to be a wayward note, but closer inspection revealed to be a card postmarked 1997, and addressed to me at my old address. It was the card from Mr. Styron. Unlike the notes, my memories of his card were perfectly clear. I remembered receiving it, and I remembered the polite but standard -thank you, no- rejection letter Mr. Styron had written: "your drawings are...original, but I really don't think I can attach my name to this sort of project. Everything that needed to be said about depression has already been said, goodbye and good luck." Feeling that I had wrestled enough demons for one day, I was going to leave the card where it was, but thought maybe it deserved a quick read and a spot in the trash with the other discards, so I fished it out of the box.

As it turned out, my perfectly clear memories of Mr. Styron's card were all complete crap. Not one thing I remembered even loosely resembled the truth. Twenty years ago Mr. Styron had taken the time to write a kind, generous reply to an unsolicited request, and what he had said was gracefully honest and thoughtful. And the part I had completely missed? It was encouraging.

It read:

Dear Ms. Ramirez: Thank you for sending me the drawings, which I found very striking and original. They go to the heart of depression with great force, conveying the terror and helplessness of the illness. I hope they will reach a large and receptive public. I've decided some time ago that what seemed necessary for me to say about depression has been said in Darkness Visible. Therefore I've pretty much refrained from further commentary in print, even if it were to accompany drawings as accomplished as yours. So I'll have to decline your invitation. But I appreciate you asking me and hope your collection has the success it deserves. Sincerely, William Styron.

For twenty years, I had firmly believed a depression-induced falsehood. I hadn't misread Mr. Styron's note. I hadn't been trying to see something that wasn't there – my misperception had not been a willful act. My eyes had lifted the words from the card exactly the way they appeared, but somewhere, on the short trip from my eyes to my mind, their meaning had been so altered I may as well have been reading them through a kaleidoscope. The only part I had been able to see accurately through the fog of depression was "So I'll have to decline". I really believed that I understood all of the ways that depression had affected me. I thought I was familiar with every facet of every symptom. But I was holding an example of something very different. It wasn't just the goings-on inside my head that depression had tampered with, it had changed how I experienced things outside my head as well. It had altered my perception of something as concrete as words on a page. It had effectively masked the good and the positive in everything, making them invisible to me. Depression had not just distorted the emotions generated within my mind, it hadn't just made me feel overwhelmingly sad or angry or indecisive or suicidal, it had systematically disrupted how I experienced all that I interacted with.

Wanting to understand how drastically depression had altered all I had taken from and put into the world, the following day I dug out my original drawings for the children's book. I needed to see them side by side with their newly rendered counterparts. Each drawing was of a child experiencing a different emotion: Alice is Angry, and terribly cross; Billy is Bored, his attention is lost, and on through the alphabet. When I fished them out of the box the previous year, I had spotted several glaring issues: errors in proportion (arms too long, legs way too short...) as well as some rather sloppy drawing technique, and a harshness in the facial expressions that left me no other option than to redraw them. Looking at them in a group with the new versions, it wasn't the drawing errors that were the most jarring, it was the faces of the children. There wasn't just a harshness about them, there was something more disturbing. It was their eyes. Their eyes were wild. They were pronounced and bulging as if something inside their heads was on the verge of bursting out. Looking at each face, I could see a perfect portrait of my own mind as it had been when I did the drawings. Agitated, angry, fearful. Depression had permeated my drawings, and I hadn't noticed. At the time they had looked fine to me...but in reality I think they had just looked familiar. I had been so saturated with the illness that everything I did dripped with it; everything I had experienced for years and years had been colored by it. Depression had drastically altered my perception of everything.

I started thinking about the really bad days that I still occasionally have. On those days every thought that I have, every thing that I do, brings with it a crushing feeling of profound sadness, as if my entire life is just one long and continuous terrible event...but on any other day the very same sort of things may stir tinges of sadness, but they also summon wonder and happiness and even joy. Depression mangles your perception so completely that there is only one view of everything you experience, and that view is dark.

And perception really is everything.

....

The following are a few of the children's book illustrations. On the off-chance you can't instantly tell which are the originals, they are on the left.

I have heard the term "I'm so depressed" used to describe the feeling of losing a favorite pair of gloves and having a cold. I've heard people who have depression described as lazy, or difficult, or unpleasant to be around. I've heard people who have died by suicide (or attempted to) described as weak. Depression isn't a cold, or some bug that lays you out for a few days. Depression is a cruel, devastating illness that removes your ability to think critically, or rationally, or even soundly. It isolates you and then feeds on your loneliness. It can manipulate your mind into believing that committing suicide is the only way to find relief from the unimaginable pain it's inflicting. It is mindfuckery in its purest form. It speaks to the depths of the misery depression brings that I avoided finishing this book for as long as I did; depression is a place that, once you have left, you never *ever* want to revisit, even if you know you won't have to stay very long.

When you have cancer, everyone rallies around you (I know this because I've had it). People bring you baked goods and do your shopping for you, they drop by bearing books and knickknacks emblazoned with inspiring messages, they arrange visits to watch movies, or drink tea or do puzzles (so many puzzles). They call to check in on a regular basis. All of which is what someone fighting depression needs: well-wishers gathering around to let them know that they are loved and valued, and would be greatly missed if they were to go away. It is not as easy as helping out a cancer patient because the cancer patient is far more likely to show their gratitude, but receiving a thank you note isn't really the point, is it? We need to start treating depression the way we do cancer (call it cancer of the mind if that makes it easier), we need to treat it as the serious and sometimes fatal illness that it is. How did it come to be that we describe people as battling cancer, but suffering from depression? Overcoming depression deserves the patina of a noble fight just as much as any other illness, and possibly more so, because it has to be waged in spite of your mind and not with the help of it.

If you know someone who is depressed, show up for them. Take them to their therapy appointments. If they don't have a therapist, help them find one. Go for a walk with them, or just hold them while they cry. Be a strong, kind, reality-based voice to counter the chaos in their head. Give them your number and assure them that they can call at any time, and answer the call when they make it no matter how late. Understand that you can't fix what they are experiencing, but you can help to tether them when they are feeling desperately unmoored.

If you are depressed or are having suicidal thoughts, tell someone, anyone: your parents, your children, your friends, that nice lady who smiles at you even when you return your library book several weeks late, and then go see your doctor and tell them. If you feel you have no one to tell, call or text the Suicide & Crisis Lifeline by dialing: 988. The people there want to talk to you. It is not hopeless. There are medications and therapies that will help you begin to feel better. Please. Tell someone.

The following pages contain my drawings of the symptoms of depression. For anyone wrestling with depression, as well as those close to them, at a point when words are desperately needed but often fail to arrive, I hope these drawings bridge the often frightening gap between the inside of a depressed mind and the world it is fighting to rejoin.

I wish you strength, resilience, and a mind free and clear, and of its own making.

Excessive
Crying

Excessive
Anger

Feelings
of Despair
and Pessimism

Feeling
Overwhelmed
or Helpless

Thoughts of
Suicide or
Suicide Attempts

Feeling Irritable
and Intolerant of
Others

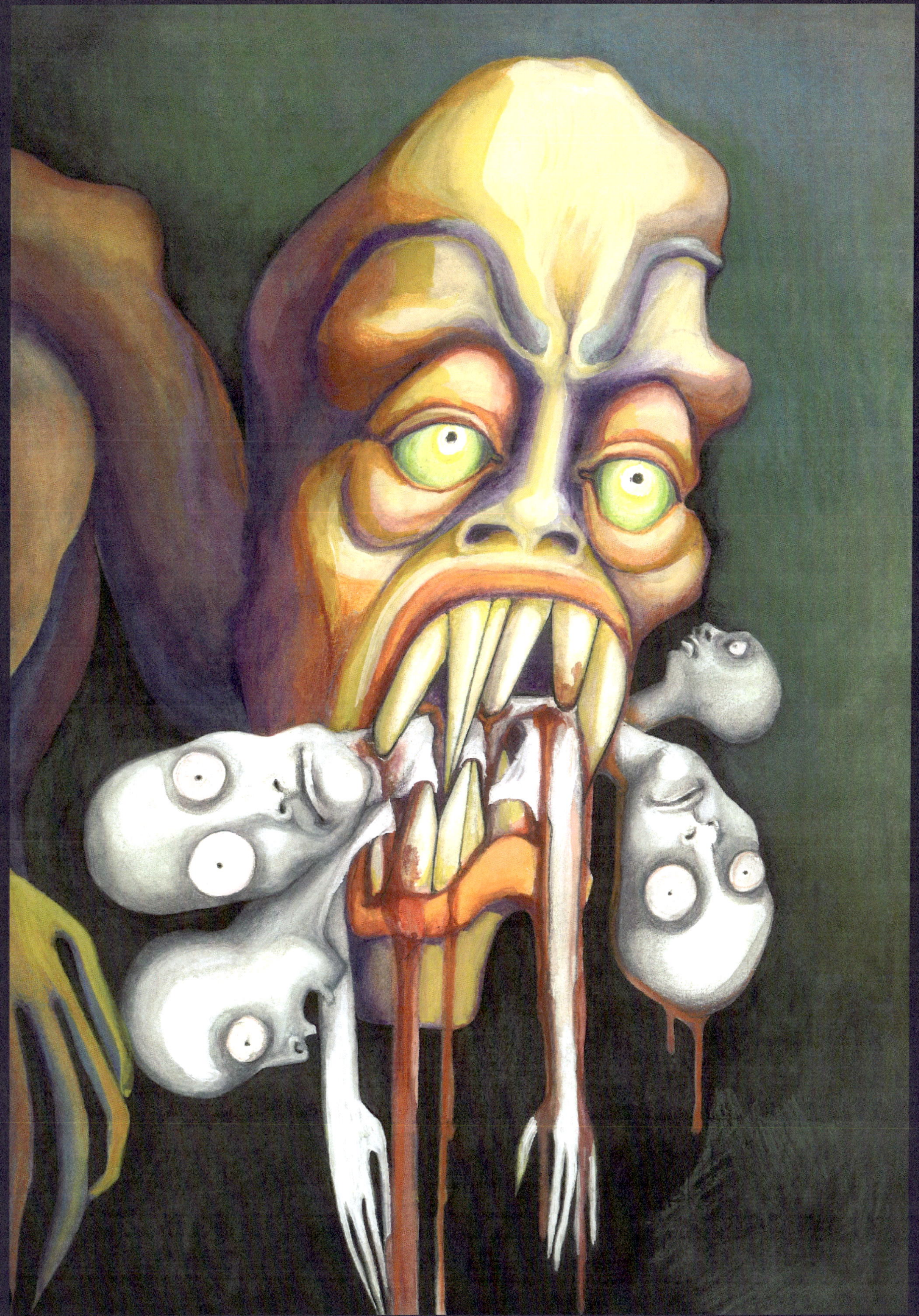

Feelings of Isolation,
Loneliness and Paranoia

Persistent
Self-Doubt

Difficulty
Concentrating
and
Making Decisions

Persistent
Sad or
Empty Mood

Feelings
of Worthlessness and
Low Self-Esteem

Feelings
of Anxiety and Worry

Feelings
of Guilt or
Shame

Insomnia,
Early Morning Waking
or Oversleeping

Loss of Appetite,
Weight Loss
or Weight Gain

Feelings
of
Hopelessness